BOOK ANALYSIS

Written by Dominique Coutant-Defer
Translated by Rose Brichard

AF131430

Matilda

BY ROALD DAHL

ROALD DAHL

BRITISH WRITER

- **Born in Wales in 1916**
- **Died in London in 1990**
- **Notable works:**
    - *Charlie and the Chocolate* Factory (1964), novel
    - *The Witches* (1983), novel
    - *Matilda* (1988), novel

Roald Dahl was born to Norwegian parents in Wales in 1916. He worked for an oil company in Africa before enlisting and joining the RAF during the Second World War. His first began writing literature targeted towards adults, but began writing children's books when he became a father. Today, he is considered the most celebrated children's author in the entire world. His books *Charlie and the Chocolate Factory, Matilda* and *The Witches* are all huge successes, and many of his works have been adapted for the screen or even the stage.

Dahl died in 1990. The 13th of September is now celebrated as Roald Dahl day in Britain, marking the author's birthday.

MATILDA

A CLASSIC TALE FOR YOUNG READERS

- **Genre:** children's novel
- **Reference edition:** Dahl, R. (1988) Matilda. [online]. Penguin: London.
- **First edition:** 1988
- **Themes:** talent, friendship, solidarity, childhood, vengeance, intelligence

Matilda first appeared in 1988, and tells the story of a gifted child named Matilda who is rejected by her vulgar parents, who have no concern for education or culture. This young girl is not only incredibly intelligent, devouring literature at an astonishing pace, but also has telekinetic powers (meaning she can make objects move with the force of her mind). She uses her powers to help her school teacher Miss Honey escape from the clutches of her aunt, the terrifying headmistress Miss Trunchbull, who has robbed her of her inheritance. The text centres around two spheres in Matilda's little world: home, dominated by television, and school, where Miss Trunchbull rules with an iron fist.

SUMMARY

A MISCHIEVOUS LITTLE GIRL

Matilda Wormwood is a little girl of 4 years old growing up in England. Her parents think of her as "nothing more than a scab" (p.6). She is highly intelligent and, having taught herself to read, she sneaks out to the library every day. The librarian is stunned by this little bookworm, and shows her how to borrow books so she might read at home. Every afternoon, Matilda goes "on olden-day sailing ships with Joseph Conrad [English writer, 2857-1924]... to Africa with Ernest Hemingway [American writer, 1899-1961] and to India with Rudyard Kipling [English writer, 1865-1936]. She travelled all over the world while sitting in her little room in an English village." (p. 15). However, Matilda is totally misunderstood by her parents, who have nowhere near their daughter's level of intelligence. She makes them furious when she asks permission to stop watching television and go to her room and read, a hobby they see no value in. This makes her furious.

One night, Mr Wormwood is so frustrated by his daughter's insatiable thirst for reading that he tears her book up before her eyes. Matilda decides to get her own back. She borrows her friend Fred's parrot and hides it in the chimney. The parrot utters the only sentence it knows - "rattle my bones" - and Matilda's family flees when she cleverly convinces them that the voice is coming from a ghost she has already heard in the house on several occasions.

Matilda's father is a car salesman, working with stolen cars to make his profits. He boasts to Matilda and her older brother about how he tricks customers into buying into this criminal enterprise - his best trick is running the cars backwards to reduce the mileage. Matilda is horrified by her father's dishonest methods and decides to play a trick on him, lining his hat with super glue the next morning. He finds the hat totally fused to his head, and is only able to get it off when Mrs Wormwood takes a pair of scissors to it, chopping off several chunks of his hair the process. He ends up with a hairdo like a monk which makes him look ridiculous, and Matilda is delighted.

One evening, Mr Wormwood asks his son to calculate the day's profit, hoping that one day he will take over the family business. Matilda does the sum in her head, which infuriates her father. Once again, Matilda decides to get her own back, and mixes his hair tonic with her mother's platinum blonde hair dye. Mrs Wormwood shrieks when she catches sight of her husband at breakfast the next morning; his black hair has turned to "dirty silver". Matilda hints that her father must have got the bottles mixed up, and Mrs Wormwood tells him that the dye is made from "a very powerful chemical" (p.47). Panicking, Mr Wormwood bellows at his wife to book him an emergency appointment to have his hair dyed black, hoping that he won't lose all of it.

SCHOOL

On her first day of school, Matilda's teacher Miss Honey warns her new class about the strict head teacher Miss

Trunchbull: "If you get on the wrong side of Miss Trunchbull she can liquidise you like a carrot in a kitchen blender" (p. 52-53). During break-time, Miss Trunchbull takes offense to one young girl's pigtails - she grabs her hair and swings the child around above her head before hurling her off into the distance. Another day, the tyrannical headmistress accuses one boy - Bruce Bogtrotter - of having stolen a slice of an enormous chocolate cake. She forces him to eat the entire cake in front of his classmates. Much to her fury, he actually succeeds, spurred on by cheering and encouragement from the other children. None of the students dare to complain, fearing the wrath of Miss Trunchbull.

Matilda quickly stands out in class, answering all the maths and literature questions right on her first try. Miss Honey recognises Matilda as a gifted child and allows her to spend class-time reading instead of sitting through lessons as her class-mates learn the basics. During break-time, Miss Honey goes to her Aunt Trunchbull's house to talk to her about Matilda. Trunchbull tells her that she has recently bought a car from Matilda's father, a likeable man who warned her about his daughter. Out of the blue she spits out that Matilda planted a stink bomb in her office, and Miss Honey's objections fall on deaf ears.

Next, Miss Honey goes to Matilda's family home to talk to her parents about their daughter and how exceptionally clever she is. Mr Wormwood is too engrossed in his soap opera to properly welcome the school teacher, but when Miss Honey mentions how Matilda loves to read, he says, "You can't make a living from sitting on your fanny and reading story-books" (p. 79). Miss Honey sees that Matilda's family has no interest in what she's trying to tell them, and she leaves, disheartened.

A HIDDEN TALENT

Little by little, Matilda and her classmates begin plotting to get back at Miss Trunchbull for humiliating and hurting her pupils. Once a week she comes to take over Miss Honey's class, and they use this as an opportunity to get up to some mischief. The day before Miss Trunchbull is due, Matilda's friend Lavender puts a newt in the head teacher's jug of water; when she arrives to terrorise the little class, she does not notice this new addition to the classroom. She begins the lesson, barking questions at the students and dishing out harsh punishments for any wrong answers, despite Miss Honey's objections. When she gets to Matilda, she tells the class that Matilda's father sold her a car which broke down after one week. "My idea of a perfect school, Miss Honey, is one that has no children in it at all" (p. 131), says the Trunchbull before reaching for a glass of water. On seeing the newt, she shrieks in terror, and quickly accuses Matilda of being responsible for this humiliation, threatening her with expulsion. Matilda is furious at the injustice of it all, and is seized by "a most extraordinary and peculiar feeling... a sense of great power... a feeling of great strength" (p. 135); she manages to tip the glass of water and the newt onto Miss Trunchbull by the power of her very mind. The headmistress storms out of the classroom. This is how Matilda discovers her telekinetic powers - her ability to move objects with her mind.

After the class, Matilda tells Miss Honey about her newly-discovered power. Miss Honey asks her to tell her exactly what happened and Matilda demonstrates her power, leaving Miss Honey amazed. She invites the girl to her own house, warning her to be careful with her mysterious abilities. Matilda arrives in Miss Honey's tiny house and realises just how poor her teacher really is. Miss Honey tells Matilda her story: all her wages go directly to her aunt who became her guardian when her father died. This aunt robbed Miss Honey of what she should have inherited on her father's death, and is none other than Miss Trunchbull herself.

Matilda promises to keep Miss Honey's secret and goes back home. As she leaves, she asks Miss Honey what her first name is, along with that of Miss Trunchbull and her late father. Miss Honey tells her: Magnus was her father, Miss Trunchbull is Agatha, and she herself is Jenny.

Little Matilda works on controlling her power for the next few days, practising with one of her father's cigars. The following Thursday when Miss Trunchbull comes to take over Miss Honey's class, she terrorises the wicked head teacher by moving a floating piece of chalk across the blackboard to write a menacing message from Magnus to Agatha. The Trunchbull is petrified and flees. Before long, she has mysteriously disappeared from the village and left everything she had to Miss Honey, who moves back into the house which is rightfully hers. Matilda visits her every day; she has lost her powers since all her mental energy is dedicated to absorbing all the knowledge available to her now that she has been moved up classes in school.

One day, Matilda's family have to flee the country, Mr Wormwood's dodgy dealings having been discovered. Matilda asks to stay with Miss Honey, and eventually her parents agree - "Why don't we let her go if that's what she wants" (p. 198).

CHARACTER STUDY

MATILDA

At the beginning of the story, Matilda Wormwood is four years old. She is a "tiny dark-haired person" (p. 10) who could speak perfectly when she was one and a half and taught herself to read when she was three. As soon as she is able to, she devours literature in secret at her local library, since her parents think reading is a waste of time. She has as little fondness for her parents as they have for her, and hates how they spend all of their time sitting in front of the television, angry with their daughter for wanting to do something different. For example, they refuse point blank to buy her any books, telling her that she doesn't need any when she has such a huge television at home. Matilda gets her own back by playing tricks on them, like the time she makes the family believe there is a ghost in the house or when she super glues her father's hat to his head. She discovers her telekinetic powers when she is five years old, and perfects her abilities to move objects with her mind. With the help of these powers and Miss Honey, she drives the terrible Miss Trunchbull out of the village forever.

MISS HONEY

Miss Honey is a teacher at the local village school, and is just like her name - sweet and mild-tempered, never raising her voice. Though she rarely smiles, she has an extraordinary talent for making all her pupils love her. She is in her early 20s, with "a lovely pale oval madonna face with blue eyes"

(p. 50). Her body too reflects her personality; she is so thin and fragile-looking that you might think she would break in two if she were to fall over. Matilda is very fond of her teacher and even writes a poem in her honour. Miss Honey also takes a real shine to Matilda. Aware that she is not receiving adequate support at home, she takes her under her wing. Miss Honey's aunt is the monstrous Miss Trunchbull, a woman who has stolen her inheritance, leaving Miss Honey forced to live in a tiny house with only the most basic of amenities.

MISS TRUNCHBULL

Miss Trunchbull also lives up to her menacing name. She is the school headmistress, and rules with an iron fist. She is described as "a fierce tyrannical monster who frightened the life out of the pupils and teachers alike" (p. 51). She hates children and is even violent towards them, capable of swinging a little girl around in the air by her pigtails and forcing a child to eat cake until he is sick. She is Miss Honey's aunt, and has robbed her niece of her rightful inheritance, leaving her to live in poverty. After Matilda terrorises Miss Trunchbull with her cunning plan and special powers, the old tyrant disappears from the village and leaves everything she has to her niece.

MR WORMWOOD

Mr Wormwood is Matilda's father, described as "a small ratty-looking man whose front teeth stuck out underneath a thin ratty moustache." (p. 17). He wears brightly-coloured checked jackets, speaks loudly and has a very high opinion of himself. He is an illegal car salesman and boasts about how he drives up sales with his criminal tricks. He has little time for Matilda and prefers his elder son, who he thinks is the cleverest of the two and hopes will one day take over the family business. He worships his television set, and spends all his time at home in front of it. He sees books and reading as worthless, except perhaps for the *Autocar* and *Motor* magazines he reads every week. His way of thinking is just as beastly as how he acts. For example, he pays little attention to Miss Honey when she comes to talk to him about Matilda, annoyed that she is interrupting his favourite soap opera.

MRS WORMWOOD

Mrs Wormwood is just as vulgar as her husband, described by Dahl as such: "She wore heavy makeup and she had one of those unfortunate bulging figures where the flesh appears to be strapped in all around the body to prevent it from falling out." (p. 21). She spends her afternoons playing bingo and leaves Matilda home alone. Neither she nor Mr Wormwood cook, so the family eat TV-dinners every night.

ANALYSIS

ACTANTIAL MODEL

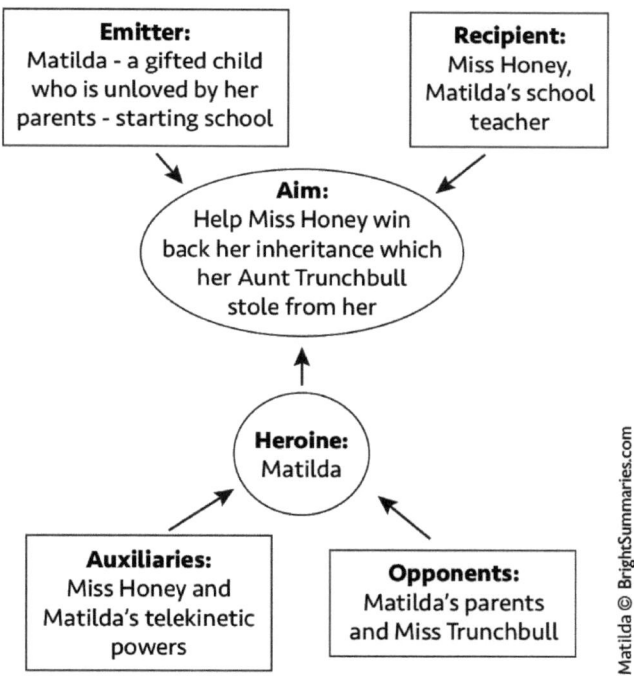

Emitter:
Matilda - a gifted child who is unloved by her parents - starting school

Recipient:
Miss Honey, Matilda's school teacher

Aim:
Help Miss Honey win back her inheritance which her Aunt Trunchbull stole from her

Heroine:
Matilda

Auxiliaries:
Miss Honey and Matilda's telekinetic powers

Opponents:
Matilda's parents and Miss Trunchbull

Matilda © BrightSummaries.com

PLOT OUTLINE

Exposition: the beginning of the story where setting and characters are established. The situation is balanced and has no reason to evolve.

- At just four years of age little Matilda, clever and imaginative, is rejected by her parents and takes refuge in her books. She is highly intelligent, but her parents are quite the opposite, chastising their daughter for her love of reading and desire to learn.

Conflict: an event changes the initial situation and acts as a catalyst which triggers the true beginning of the plot.

- When Matilda starts school, she realises she has telekinetic powers during a class with the tyrannical Miss Trunchbull.

Development: The events which occur as a result of the rising action or actions taken by the hero to resolve the problem.

- Matilda's teacher Miss Honey, whom she is very fond of, tells her that Miss Trunchbull is in fact her aunt, and that she has robbed her of her inheritance. Matilda uses her extraordinary powers to terrify the headmistress into fleeing the village and leaving everything to Miss Honey.

Falling Action: The development comes to an end and the plot moves towards its resolution.

- Matilda's family is forced to leave the country due to Mr Wormwood's dodgy dealings.

Resolution: The end of the story where a new situation,

stable like the exposition, is established.

- Mr and Mrs Wormwood agree to let Matilda stay with Miss Honey.

A NOVEL FOR YOUNG READERS

Aside from traditional children's tales like the fairy tales by the Brothers Grimm or Perrault, young readers have a whole genre dedicated to them: children's literature. This genre developed considerably during the 19th century, when books like Charles Dickens' *Oliver Twist* and Hector Malot's *Nobody's Boy* first appeared.

Children's literature has several common characteristics, all of which can be found in Roald Dahl's *Matilda*:

- The text focusses on one or several children. In *Matilda*, the young reader's attention is focussed on the gifted little Matilda and her classmates;
- Since the protagonists are children, young readers identify more easily both with the characters and with the situations presented;
- Adults are often shown to be inferior to the children involved. In this case, Dahl presents a particularly harsh vision of the adult world, with Matilda's parents being rude, loud and nasty to their daughter. Miss Trunchbull too is described as a monster, and shows her sadistic nature in how she treats her pupils. Only Miss Honey, who is adored by all her pupils, shows herself to be worth the children's time.
- Themes specific to children's literature are explored.

Friendship, solidarity among children (in the face of Miss Trunchbull's tyrannical reign, for example), parents and the difficult relationships they might have with their offspring are all themes which are present in *Matilda*. Matilda's parents literally do not like their daughter, and she gets her own back by playing clever tricks on them, for example convincing them that they have a ghost in their house;

- The story has a moral. Stories for young readers often aim to transmit certain moral values through engaging the reader in feelings of empathy with the characters. In *Matilda*, the author shows that bad people are always punished and good people get what they deserve in the end; the wicked Miss Trunchbull is forced to flee the town, while Miss Honey and Matilda live happily ever after;
- The writing style caters to a younger audience. The novel features a lot of dialogue, and though it is relatively long, it is divided into short chapters which are more digestible chunks for the younger reader's attention span.

We want to hear from you!
Leave a comment on your online library
and share your favourite books on social media!

FURTHER READING

REFERENCE EDITION

- Dahl, R. (1988) *Matilda*. London: Penguin. (illustrated by Quentin Blake).

ADAPTATION

- *Matilda*. (1996) [Film]. Danny De Vito. Dir. USA: TriStar Pictures.
- *Matilda the Musical*. (2013) [Stage musical]. Dennis Kelly. UK.

MORE FROM BRIGHTSUMMARIES.COM

- Reading guide - *Charlie and the Chocolate Factory* by Roald Dahl

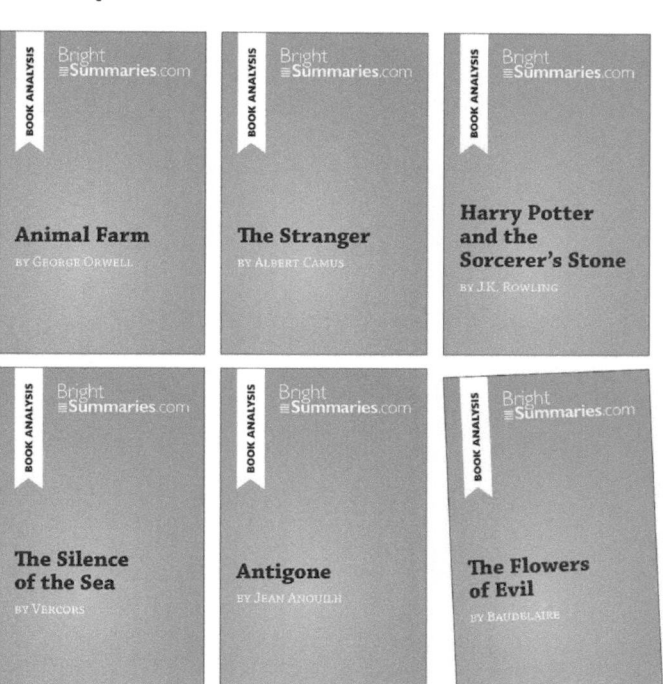